A SCHOOL LEADER'S GUIDE TO DEALING WITH DIFFICULT PARENTS

This new supplement to the bestselling *Dealing with Difficult Parents, Second Edition* is designed to help you with the specific challenges you face as a school leader when dealing with parents. The main book, *Dealing with Difficult Parents, Second Edition*, shows how your teachers and other educators can communicate with parents more effectively. With this new supplement, you'll learn how you, as a leader, can—and must—support and coach teachers along the way.

Topics covered include how to . . .

♦ Make sure your teachers understand the families they're dealing with;

♦ Help your teachers communicate effectively with parents by being positive and proactive, so problems don't escalate to the main office;

♦ Establish expectations for dealing with parents, so teachers understand how to be appropriate even when a parent is not;

- Ensure your teachers feel supported by you when they're dealing with difficult parents; and
- Help teachers become more confident and empowered in challenging situations.

With these practical books, you'll be able to get parents on your side so they can become a positive force in your school's success.

A School Leader's Guide to Dealing with Difficult Parents

Todd Whitaker and Douglas J. Fiore

Routledge
Taylor & Francis Group

NEW YORK AND LONDON

First published 2016
by Routledge
711 Third Avenue, New York, NY 10017

and by Routledge
2 Park Square, Milton Park, Abingdon, Oxon, OX14 4RN

Routledge is an imprint of the Taylor & Francis Group, an informa business

© 2016 Taylor & Francis

The right of Todd Whitaker and Douglas J. Fiore to be identified as authors of
this work has been asserted by them in accordance with sections 77 and 78 of the
Copyright, Designs and Patents Act 1988.

Library of Congress Cataloging-in-Publication Data
A catalog record for this book has been requested

ISBN: 978-1-138-96345-0 (pbk)
ISBN: 978-1-315-65877-3 (ebk)

Typeset in Palatino
by Apex CoVantage, LLC

Printed and bound in the United States of America by Sheridan Books, Inc. (a Sheridan Group Company).

Contents

About the Authors

Dr. Todd Whitaker is a professor of education leadership at Indiana State University in Terre Haute, Indiana. Prior to coming to Indiana, he coached and taught at the middle and high school levels in Missouri. Following his teaching experience, he served as a middle school, junior high, and high school principal. In addition, Dr. Whitaker served as middle school coordinator for new middle schools.

Dr. Whitaker has been published in the areas of principal effectiveness, teacher leadership, change, and staff motivation. He has written 40 books including *What Great Teachers Do Differently, Dealing with Difficult Teachers, Motivating & Inspiring Teachers* and *What Connected Educators Do Differently*. He is a highly sought after speaker for educators.

Todd is married to Beth, a former teacher and principal, who serves as director of the Faculty Center for Teaching Excellence at Indiana State. Beth and Todd have three children, Katherine, Madeline, and Harrison.

Dr. Douglas J. Fiore is currently the interim provost at Ashland University in Ashland, Ohio. Prior to coming to Ohio, he served in faculty and leadership roles at Virginia State University, Virginia Commonwealth University, and the University of West Georgia. Dr. Fiore began his educational career teaching at the elementary school level in Indiana. Following his teaching experience, he served as an elementary school principal in two Indiana schools.

Dr. Fiore has been published in the areas of school-community relations, leadership theory, principal effectiveness, and school culture and has presented at numerous national and state conferences. He is the author of eight books including the best-selling textbook, *School-Community Relations,* as well as

Introduction to Educational Administration: Standards, Theories and Practice, and *Six Types of Teachers: Recruiting, Retaining and Mentoring the Best.*

Doug is the proud father of three daughters, Meagan, Amy, and Katherine.

Introduction

Why This Book?

It has been an interesting journey to write this book. The first edition of *Dealing with Difficult Parents* (2001) was written for all educators. We intended to meet the needs of all readers, whether the reader was a first-year classroom teacher or a veteran administrator. The response to the book was tremendous, which has been very satisfying. However, there was always a gnawing feeling in us that by trying to serve all educators, maybe we were not best serving anyone. After years of wrestling with a plan for improvement, we decided to develop a separate book for school leaders, especially for principals, on working with challenging parents.

Our reasons were two fold. The first is that many times principals have to deal with situations that they were not directly involved in. For example, they were not on the school bus when an incident occurred, and the bus driver may have only a "best guess" version as to what happened, yet the principal must still decide on an appropriate discipline. Or the principal has to determine the most fitting action to take involving a teacher and a student. What makes it doubly challenging is that this could have been initiated because of an office referral from an upset teacher or a phone call from an angry or frustrated parent. Obviously, teachers get their fair share of surprise phone calls or emails from students' upset family members, but typically they have a much higher direct knowledge or role in the situation.

School leaders have a different water to navigate when it comes to receiving or initiating contact with difficult parents. Though a principal may happen onto a fight or other school situation that they have to deal with (and that leads them to communicate with the home), a great majority of these cases involve indirect involvement and thus need a different approach than the classroom teacher may utilize when dealing with such a parent. Being able to have specific language to use with parents, whether it involves you delivering bad news or defusing volatility that is brought your way, is an essential part of being an effective principal. Many times the approach and verbiage needed is similar to what a teacher should use but can vary enough that we felt there should be a separate guide for assisting with this.

The other area that is dramatically different for administrators than it is for teachers is the need to be able to successfully defend faculty and staff when they are being accused of a wrongdoing by an angry or upset parent. Teachers often have to defend themselves and their actions; they are able to explain through firsthand knowledge the rationale behind decisions and choices that they made in leading their class. The principals do not have this information at the ready. This can involve situations where the parent is directly approaching the teacher and we hear about it either prior to or after the fact, and we need to be supportive of the accused employee. A similar need arises when we are dealing with parents themselves, and they are attacking an undeserving staff member. These things can occur when we contact a parent about a classroom discipline situation or when we receive unsolicited calls or emails from an unhappy family member.

One other purpose of this special book for administrators is to help principals and other educational leaders build the skills of their staff so their staff becomes more confident in dealing with challenging parents. Without building others' skills, leaders could consistently be stuck in a defensive and protective mode and end up doing a disproportionate amount of interacting with parents. When we build the skills of others, it can greatly assist in creating healthier home-school relationships and thus can create a much richer culture of caring in our schools. If we do not figure out ways to empower others, we keep them in a much more weakened state than they should be. The result of this is that the principal ends up being in the middle of many situations that would be more effectively resolved by direct teacher-parent communication. However, if we do not build the teacher skills correctly, then we will have plenty of practice defending ineffective approaches.

As you read this book, keep in mind that we use two terms in the broadest of senses. One is that we call everyone who might represent or support a student a "parent." We felt that for readability, it was easier to say "parent" than to say parent/step parent/grandparent/guardian/foster parent, etc. This is not to desensitize us to the myriad of backgrounds and challenges students come to us from. It is also not to rank the people according to importance. It is really just to make the book smoother to the audience. We have great faith that you will have an awareness of and sensitivity to each situation your students are in.

The other term is "teacher," which we use to describe everyone in your school. It is important to support and build the skills of everyone who works with the young people in your building. Whether the person drives a bus, sweeps the floors, is a social worker, counselor, teacher, instructional assistant or anything else you can think of, that person is functioning as a teacher. We have great faith that principals and all educators can use whatever term they need to describe themselves and their colleagues. Rather than trying to list all possible occupational titles, it seemed to be more user-friendly to have people fill in the blanks as needed.

Also, keep in mind that in this book, we are talking about the most challenging of parents. Normal approaches work with regular people. However, with a few individuals, it takes a special touch. Communicating with caring and responsible parents who can view their own children in a somewhat objective way is not too difficult. Dealing with those few individuals who at times struggle with their own sense of right and wrong can be quite a challenge. That is what this resource is for. Good reading and thanks for choosing to make a difference.

1

Understanding Is Not an Excuse

In *Dealing with Difficult Parents* (Whitaker, 2002), there is a great deal of information on the factors that affect today's parents and cause such a seemingly large number of dysfunctional families—and thus students—to arrive at our schools each day. Understanding today's families can help us be empathetic to the needs of the students we work with each day. It is equally as important for you, as building leaders, to be familiar with the current challenges parents deal with, challenges that our generation—whatever that even means—may not have faced.

However, one key point is that leaders must help their staff members comprehend the difference between *understanding* the background of the students we have in our classes, cafeteria, and school buses, and *using this knowledge as an excuse* to not be effective in teaching and reaching our students.

Provide Perspective

Many times, we compare ourselves to others. We wonder why overweight people don't exercise as much as we do, or we lament that we do not have the metabolism that our trimmer friends do. We assign blame in some situations and make excuses for ourselves in others. This is human nature, to some degree, but we must be careful to make sure it does not prevent us from doing what we can do to make a difference.

So often, we compare ourselves to the side that best proves our point. We will say we are underpaid compared to . . . and of course, we only do a comparison with those who get paid more than we do. A situation occurred recently where school district employees were threatening a strike because a neighboring district got paid more than they did. I believe that teachers are not nearly paid their worth, but in this situation the irony was the district that was complaining was the second highest compensated in the state. Their neighboring district was the only one that had higher salaries.

A leader has to help provide a proper perspective by making sure that we all are aware of the many positives we have in our school. We can assure you that the parents in your school do the best they know how. This does not mean that they do the best you know how or that they do the best that your college-educated teachers who may have come from supportive, two-parent families know how. It just means that in their current dynamic—and it may be incredibly dysfunctional—they are doing the best they can. They unquestionably love their own children; they just may not know what to do to actually show it at times. Parents who mistreat their children are often times behaving exactly as their parents (if they had them) behaved toward them when they were little. This does not mean they *should* be doing this—of course not. It does mean that they may not realize what they are doing is inappropriate or even more likely, they do not know what the proper alternatives are.

Part of a teacher and principal's role is to help teach parents proper skills when the opportunity arises. *Dealing with Difficult Parents* and this book both have language you can use to help with this teaching process.

Additionally, remember that parents bring the best children they have to your schools and classrooms each day. They do not keep the good ones at home with them; they go ahead and bring all four. Our challenge is to make sure everyone in our school does what is best for each of these students. And many times, we must remember that just like the parents, all of our faculty and staff members do the best they know how. If we have adults who work in our school who are not doing what is right, we must teach them a better way. Then we can hold them accountable for doing so.

Reframing

Perspective is essential. According to the National Center for Educational Statistics, School Nutrition Association (2013), approximately 48 percent of students in the United States are on free and reduced lunch. States vary from a low (New Hampshire) of 24 percent to a high (Washington, D.C.) of 73 percent. Now, knowing where your school falls—and it may be 100 percent—do you and your faculty compare yourselves to schools who have a lower socio-economic population or to one with a higher socio-economic population? As I work with schools and districts around the world, leaders will tell me, "We are very fortunate we have only a 75 percent free- and reduced-lunch population," because they are comparing themselves to others who are not as well off. By the same token, other leaders will say, "We really have challenging students. Our free- and reduced-lunch rate is up to 19 percent."

This is not to make light of anyone's situation at all, quite the opposite. Sometimes we look at those around us who are more fortunate and lament, and other times we may look in the rearview mirror and compare ourselves to what we remember the "good old days" to be like.

There are many factors besides poverty and single-family home makeup that bring challenges for educators. Sometimes we struggle with parents because they are too busy and other times we have parents who continually hover over their children and our schools because they are not busy enough. Too much of a good thing is still too much. The point is that it is up to a leader to continually put things in a light that allows us to continue to move forward and maybe even see how fortunate we are to have the population we do. It is easy to compare ourselves to those who are luckier than we are; however, at times it is essential that we weigh against those who are not, in order to provide the right frame of mind for us to make a difference with the young people in our schools and classrooms.

We cannot control many of the outside influences that our students face, but we can sway the way we view them. It is interesting: The best teachers know more about the background of their students and yet they never use these demographics as an excuse. Less effective staff members barely know the students and yet they seldom hesitate to use these things as a rationale for why they cannot teach a challenging individual. The school leader has to consistently work to make sure that everyone in the building takes a positive view of the school environment as well as of the young people we work with. The students deserve it. It is the least we can do.

Chapter 1 Recap

♦ Make sure your teachers keep the proper perspective on the families they're dealing with—but don't let them use their understanding of these families as an excuse for not dealing with them effectively.

♦ Reframe situations as needed to help your teachers see the positives in the school and in the students and parents.

2

Identify the Problem Before You Try to Solve It

One of the first challenges we face when we are dealing with difficult people is to make sure we know who is the difficult one. Often times, we must pull up a mirror to find the true source of the problem. As leaders, it is essential we self-reflect, but it is equally critical that we help others in our organization do the same. We focus on internal people first simply because they are the ones we are most responsible for, and they are the ones we have the most ability to influence. Everyone in a school can *wish* all of the parents were reasonable and had a high level of skills. Everyone in a school *can* be reasonable and have a high level of skills. That is why this must come first.

If, as leaders, we continually find ourselves having to defend inappropriate practices, our job becomes incredibly and increasingly stressful. And it is deservedly so. Our task as leaders is to make sure we do what is right so we reduce the number of challenges. It is also much easier to defend and support correct practices than it is to rationalize incorrect acts. Everything must start there.

Teach Rather Than Tell

As a school leader, one discovery you may have had is that many teachers are hesitant with or even afraid of parents.

There may be multiple reasons for this, and some of them are very good ones. Staff may have had parents be verbally rude when they call them with less than good news. Teachers at different points in their careers have had parents yell or cuss (or worse) at them when they are upset. Whether through email, phone, or in person, many educators wind up being blamed for a student's academic or interpersonal struggles.

Some of teachers' hesitation or fear comes from personal experience, and some of it derives from their teaching colleagues telling their own war stories of parent interactions they have had or have heard about. It is imperative that a school leader work to build the skills of all staff members and especially help new teachers begin their careers with an effective skill set involving parent contact.

Dealing with Difficult Parents provides a stem that teachers can use to start all of their contacts with parents. Using something like, "Hi Mrs. Johnson, this is Mary Smith, Kevin's math teacher. I am sorry to bother you at work . . . " Giving teachers a consistent way to start each contact—whether it is to deliver good news or bad—is a powerful support mechanism.

Word for Word

One of the primary reasons for writing these books about parents is to provide educators with specific language to use. A building leader could put together a "cheat sheet" of phrases that everyone could have on or near their phone and computer. It is similar to what I did in high school. Before I would nervously call up a girl and ask her on a date, I always had a crib sheet of notes so that after I would vomit, I knew what to say next.

Role Play

It's like the old saying, "If we don't model what we teach, then we are teaching something else." Faculty meetings, new teacher orientations, and other settings could be ideal times to demonstrate how to speak to parents. Then have people role-play and practice specific scenarios that are all too common in your school. Practicing them in a setting like this, so they can hear tone and manner as well as specific terminology, can go a long way to providing support.

Recordings

Many schools now record conversations, just like your cable provider and credit card companies do when you call them. If there are some conversations that are particularly beneficial as learning opportunities (or maybe even humorous depending on the situation), they could be shared with faculty and staff so they have a more precise "how-to" when having interactions like this. The same thing could apply to sharing email responses, etc. when appropriate. You could delete names if needed, but the context might be very beneficial.

Keep It Public

If you want to teach your office staff and other building staff how to defuse volatile parents, and if you want to demonstrate appropriate tone and manner so your staff can manage these upset people themselves (so the upset people don't wind up in your office!), have the conversation in front of your employees. They will quickly learn how you do not rattle, and they will be more able to emulate the body language, facial expression, and voice level you want them to use when they see it themselves. Once they have caught on themselves, you can proceed to move people to a more private setting without an audience.

Another method you can try, especially with new teachers, is to have them come into your office when you call a parent. They get to hear the sentence stem you use to begin the phone call, as well as the professional manner in which you deal with the parent. This method can be doubly helpful if it is a particularly volatile parent that they get to see and hear you defuse appropriately.

Establish Expectations

There are three things that should never take place in a school. Educators—whether they are a bus driver, cook, teacher, or principal—should never argue, yell, or use sarcasm. The books *What Great Teachers Do Differently* (Whitaker, 2011) and *What Great Principals Do Differently* (Whitaker, 2011) expand on exactly why these things should never occur in a school, or home for that matter. What is important to understand in this book's context is that arguing, yelling, and using sarcasm escalate behaviors. When they occur in the classroom or in the principal's office, they actually promote inappropriate behaviors on the part of a student. We must help teachers and other staff members keep in mind that they cannot behave in a way toward students that they would not accept from the students themselves. It is essential that a principal assist all teachers to understand this, starting at the first faculty meeting of the year when these behaviors have not yet occurred.

This guideline also applies when working with parents. Arguing, yelling, and using sarcasm cannot occur when educators—and especially the principal—interact with parents, regardless of the manner in which the parents approach us. Please make sure you help everyone in your school understand that classroom management has a lot more to do with class than it does management. We cannot out-smart-alec a smart-alec, and we must make sure we do not even attempt this impossible feat.

We Must Ask for Their Help

It is important that parents always feel like they are in the loop with a school and especially with things that involve their own child. What can be difficult is that the more of a pain a parent is the less fun it is to keep them in the loop. However, remember that we also keep them informed so parents can shoulder some of the responsibility in correcting and improving their child's behavior.

One way to do this is to call the parent and ask for his or her help. This is even more important for a teacher to do before the student reaches the point of an office referral on minor repetitive misbehavior. If the first time parents are contacted is *after* their child is receiving discipline, they can ask, and rightfully so, "Why didn't I know?" Let's use a silly example of a student not bringing a pencil to class six times. (Sadly, this is not silly in all classrooms and schools.)

If the administrator receives an office referral that says, "Bryan has not brought a pencil to class six times," and you call the parents to share this, they will often respond by questioning why they were not informed (especially if any kind of consequence is involved). Under this circumstance, you may feel defensive. And the reason you might is because the parents have a good point. Why didn't they know?

So if at the first faculty meeting of the year, you can teach your teachers to contact parents and ask for their help *before* a student is sent to the office for nickel and dime repetitive behavior, it can help change the tone. If a teacher calls and says, "Hi Mrs. Johnson, I am sorry to bother you at work. I was wondering if I could get your help with something." Then 95 percent of the time a parent will respond affirmatively. The 5 percent of parents we tend to be most hesitant in contacting are likely to ask, "What do you want help with?" The teacher could say, "Bryan has not brought a pencil to class three times. I do not want him to fall behind in his work and I do not want to get the office involved. I'd appreciate it if you could visit with him tonight to make sure he has a pencil tomorrow, because I do not want him to fall behind in his work and I do not want to get the office involved."

Keep in mind that the parents also do not want him to fall behind in his work, and they especially do not want to get the office involved. No one is in trouble yet. We are trying to prevent problems rather than respond to them.

Now if the behavior persists and would result in an office referral when the principal calls the parent, then the conversation can start like this, "Hi Mrs. Johnson, I am sorry to bother you at work. I know Mrs. Smith, Bryan's science teacher, contacted you about him not bringing a pencil to class three more times and as a result . . ." The difference is the parents now have some of the responsibility because the teacher asked for their help prior to the office contacting them.

Now the pencil example may be silly, but there are chronic problems like students repeatedly talking out of turn, inappropriate outbursts, and so on that may result in office contact for a student. Regardless of the repeated minor infraction, taking a preventative approach can greatly shift the dynamic. However, we need to help our teachers understand why and how to do this in a preventative way prior to any consequences for the student.

Teachers Who Are Wrong Versus Parents Who Are Right

In other parts of this book and in *Dealing with Difficult Parents*, we discuss how to handle things if we are wrong. This section is actually not related to that. Instead, this is a big picture issue about our school. We have to decide as leaders what issues we face and what issues we want to face. This may not even make sense at first glance, but one of my mantras as a principal was that *I would rather deal with a teacher who is wrong rather than deal with a parent who is right*.

My mantra was not about an isolated situation. Defending an effective teacher who errs is actually pretty easy. Typically, the teacher wants to repair and/or resolve the situation and make amends with the student, parent, or anyone who may have been affected or offended. Even supporting an ineffective teacher is not too challenging if he or she is willing to try to make any effort to show empathy or regret. Instead, what the mantra refers to is the teacher who consistently treats students inappropriately, regularly behaves unprofessionally, or all too often makes poor choices in professional actions. This is typically not a teacher who only receives complaints from the usually whiny parent. Instead, it refers to the teacher who has challenging relationships with even the cooperative parents and responsible students.

If you find yourself regularly having to defend a staff member, and you feel that you may be on the side of wrong quite frequently, then ask yourself if maybe your focus should be on the staff member rather than the parent. Always keep in mind that if you have even a few difficult teachers and they are allowed to continually approach others inappropriately, you are going to be blessed with difficult parents this year, and the next, and the next . . .

Sometimes it comes down to this: Would I rather deal with an ineffective staff member though it may be uncomfortable for a while, or would I prefer to deal with difficult parents on an ongoing basis? The reason the book *Dealing with Difficult Teachers* (Whitaker, 2014) has three editions is that it is the single most difficult thing a principal has to do. But if we do not do so when appropriate and do not do so correctly, we may find ourselves in consistently undefendable and defensive situations with parents, and there is nothing fun about that.

As an example, let's go back to the situation regarding not having a pencil. If there is a teacher or two in your building who does not contact parents and ask for their help, we must figure out ways to approach them, or the teachers who *are* doing the contacting will be disappointed in the lack of follow through by the leader, not by the teacher. After the first time or two of a teacher not calling in this preventative manner, we can remind them of the importance of it, and we can review the language to use. However, at some point, we need to switch from asking, "Did you get a chance to contact the parent?" to asking, "How did it go when you contacted the parent?" This puts much more of a responsibility on the teacher because by now, you know they are intentionally refusing rather than wondering if they do not know how. It is reasonable to eventually tell and expect the teacher that he or she needs to contact the parent and ask for help before you will take a supportive action.

Make Sure Our Practices and Rules Make Sense

In Chapter 12 of *Dealing with Difficult Parents*, we discuss how teachers can ensure that their rules and procedures make sense in the classroom. This same thing applies on a school-wide basis. You do not want to have to support teachers who are consistently wrong, and you do not want to support rules that are not logical. Examining our school and district practices as well as our own actions is an essential part of our role. It is very difficult to make sense out of something that inherently doesn't make sense.

Chapter 2 Recap

♦ Self-reflect on your own dealings with parents and encourage teachers to do the same. Are the parents really the difficult ones?

♦ Help your teachers learn to communicate effectively with parents. For example, give teachers a script for how to start each parent call. Role-play situations with teachers and record conversations as necessary.

♦ Have teachers watch your own dealings with difficult parents so they can learn from your example.

♦ Establish expectations for dealing with parents. For example, no matter how rude parents are, teachers should never yell back or use sarcasm.

♦ Suggest that teachers ask parents for help dealing with certain situations. Asking for help will make parents feel involved and will create a more positive tone.

♦ If you find yourself constantly defending teachers who are in the wrong, put more responsibility on them to improve rather than continually support them.

3

Supporting Your Staff

One of the biggest challenges principals face is supporting teachers and other staff members when they come under criticism of parents. Truly, this can be a make-or-break issue for the credibility of the building leader in the eyes of the faculty. If this is done correctly, it can give you a wide swath of influence when dealing with other issues or asking teachers to take on essential additional leadership roles in the school. If this is handled incorrectly, it can very quickly shatter the trust level and influence a principal has with the professionals who are in the school.

Supporting teachers when they are under fire from parents is similar to how we must support teachers in the area of student discipline. If we are seen as weak, non-supportive, or even afraid, it can send shivers of impact down the hallways and into the teachers' lounge. Let's compare it to support regarding student discipline. Principals will get a new job and then share with me that the teachers wanted someone older, or someone of a different gender, or someone local, or someone with more experience, etc. I always reassure them by saying, "All of that matters until the first student is sent to the office." When a teacher sends a student to the office for discipline and the teacher feels supported, it does not matter at all what the background of the administrator is. When a teacher sends a student to the office for discipline and the teacher does *not* feel supported, it does not matter what the administrator's background is. This exact same comparison applies to feeling administrative support when dealing with parent issues.

Feel Supported

You may have noticed the term "feel supported" in that section. Please note that it does not just say the teacher is supported. This does not mean that the staff members will not be supported. That is a given. But a key component of this, which is too often overlooked, is that teachers also want to "feel" supported. Let's look at an example involving student discipline.

If a student is sent to the office for a minor infraction and is assigned two hours of after-school detention, this is an example of a leader supporting the teacher. However, if we do not communicate to the teacher what we did as a consequence, and possibly explain how that decision was made, the teacher may not feel supported because he or she might not even know what occurred. Instead, after assigning two hours of detention, the administrator could personally go to the teacher, explain the consequence, share what was said to the parent when they called, and tell the teacher "Let me know how he behaves when he returns to class tomorrow. We will not tolerate this type of behavior in our school and in your classroom." Then the teacher is much more likely to "feel" supported then in the previous non-communicative two-hour detention assignment. Never underestimate the power of this emotional reassurance. It is a critical component and should be kept in mind when supporting teachers in any way, but especially when supporting them with students and parents.

The Gift of Confidence

One of the most powerful gifts a leader can give others is the gift of confidence. Support is one way that this can be given. Another essential way to help others have confidence is by demonstrating that you have it yourself. When a teacher tells you that Mrs. Fireball, a volatile parent, is on her way to school, how do you react? If you tense up, so that it can be easily noticed by the teacher, potentially you have taken away the teacher's confidence. You have validated that teacher's fear of Mrs. Fireball. At the other end of the spectrum, if you smile and say professionally, "It's always a treat to see Mrs. Fireball," you may help the teacher relax simply because you had a relaxed response. Being aware of how you come across and how you deal with stressful situations will have a ripple effect—either way—on your school. Keep in mind that when it comes to leadership of a school, calm is good. Let's take a look at something that you can do regularly that will instill confidence in those we lead. It is also something that can be taught to those who are in our school.

Line in the Sand

When we interact with people who like to intimidate, especially if they do so with anger, we should remember that they want one of two things. They would like us to respond with fear or react with anger. Either one works well for them. Picture two people face to face. One is emotionally launching toward the other. The aggressor is ready for the other person to either wither back or launch right back. Neither of these responses is appropriate, and more importantly, neither of these responses is effective. The people who act so aggressively are drawing a figurative line in the sand. They are hoping we back away so they get a bigger swath of territory, or they are hoping we cross that line so they have permission to respond with "no holds barred" on their part. Rather than choosing either of these approaches, let's choose something that will keep them off guard. It is something we call the "sidle up."

What this means is anytime we approach a potentially volatile person, rather than interacting with them face to face—i.e., line in the sand—we should approach them from the side, just like they are an old friend. When an angry or intimidating parent stomps into your office, do not sit on the other side of the desk. To them this is a line in the sand. Instead, move around to the other side of the desk and sit right next to them like they were the nicest parent in the school.

Your first thought might be, "I would feel terribly uncomfortable doing this!" Of course you would. It is never fun interacting with a bossy and unreasonable person. However, keep in mind that if you stay across a desk or table from them, you will still feel uncomfortable. You know why? Because they are still bossy and unreasonable. But the benefit of moving is very simple. When you sit next to them, they also feel some of this discomfort. So rather than you sitting across from them helping them to form their desired line in the sand, sit next to them and then both of you can feel awkward instead of it just being you. This may sound strange, but try it and you will find out how powerful it is. It is very disarming for the most challenging parents and others whom we interact with.

This same principle applies if you are supervising a basketball game, play, or concert. If there is a challenging parent misbehaving in the stands, be very friendly and go sit right next to them. Not only will this likely knock them off their game, it will help everyone whom they are making uncomfortable because you are not acting afraid, so that means they do not need to be afraid either. While there, if they continue to be disruptive or disrespectful, you can nicely and professionally say, "I hate to tell you this, but if you stand up again I will have to have you escorted out of the gym. I am so sorry, but if you stand up again I will have to have you leave." They are the only person who needs to hear this. There is no need for an announcement. By doing this, you have clearly laid out an expectation for the only person who needs it. Now, if they do it again, both of you know what the consequences are.

By approaching difficult people in this manner and eliminating the line in the sand, you take some of the steam out of these agitators. At the same time, you are giving confidence to your staff because you're demonstrating how they can be professional and calm around volatile people whom they might fear.

Chapter 3 Recap

♦ Make sure teachers "feel" supported by you when they're dealing with difficult students and parents.

♦ Help teachers become more confident in their dealings with challenging parents. Do this by modeling how you are confident with parents yourself.

♦ Eliminate the line in the sand with volatile parents.

4

Be Aware of What You Don't Know

When I was an assistant principal dealing with discipline, many times I found myself talking with parents about issues that I did not observe firsthand. Regardless, I still had to figure out a way to work effectively with the situation. One way that worked was to be honest with the parent. I would often say, "One of the tough things about this situation, Mr. Martinez, is that for the two people talking right now, neither one of us was there." This would allow me to focus on what we did have control over. We could then center on the "what can we do to make sure this does not occur again" conversation.

This can help tremendously to defuse the situation. The parents may arrive with great confidence because their child, "told them the truth," but once you reduce their knowledge base by identifying the fact that neither of you were there, it can soften the dialogue a great deal.

If the parents were very belligerent, then I would shift the conversation to something that I did know about. For example, if parents insisted that this teacher was picking on their son and that their child was wrongly sent to the office, I would steer the dialogue from something I did not have firsthand knowledge of to something that I *did* have personal awareness of. The conversation may take a turn in this direction:

> One of the tough things about this situation, Mr. Martinez, is that for the two people talking right now, neither one of us was there. And obviously, neither one of us can sort out exactly what did occur. However, I want to share with you what I saw your son do in Mrs. Martin's class last Wednesday. I saw him out of his seat, disrupting other students, throwing his pencil at someone else, and poking at three students with scissors. And Mrs. Martin did not send him to the office that day. You need to know I thought his behavior was so inappropriate that she should have. However, if today his behavior was so bad that she did send him to the office, it only makes me shudder to think exactly what his behavior was today.

What I was doing with this conversation was reestablishing control of the discussion. Rather than focusing on something that I did not have firsthand knowledge about (today's behavior), I centered on something that I did observe that was inappropriate. Not only did this take the focus off of this disputed situation, it also defended the teacher by indicating that she was more tolerant and fair than I would have been.

Again, you need to be selective in using this approach, but in very challenging situations, this is a powerful tool. Another example is that you could contact parents regarding their child bullying other students. Your contact this time may be about a reported behavior. However, if the parents choose to be uncooperative, you might be able to gain control of the situation by referring to a bullying situation that you did observe the same student do, but that the bullying victim did not report. Thus, the latest situation must have been even worse for the student (victim) to come to you and complain this time. Not only will this type of approach generally put you in control of the discussion, but it may also give you a little bit of a confidence boost and help you gain more control over your emotions.

Who Do We Call First?

In Chapter 8 of *Dealing with Difficult Parents*, we describe a situation where a teacher may feel that their class is out of control, and it has evolved to the point of needing to contact parents. Let's go through that example from the point of view of the principal.

There are times when teachers may frantically come to you and exclaim that their class is completely out of control. The first thing you should do is help them reflect and clarify by asking them, "Your class is completely out of control?" When they answer affirmatively, calmly and professionally rephrase, "Every student is out of control?" Once again, they will likely breathlessly respond positively. At that point, take a look at their class list and ask if the nicest student in the class is out of control. They most likely will say no. Then ask about the second nicest student, etc. It turns out that there are five students out of control. Well, clearly that is a problem as we only have four corners in our room! Well, let's imagine that we have tried everything and finally we decide to call parents. How many parents should we call?

If you read *Dealing with Difficult Parents*, you may recall that we should call one student—and rather than it being the leader, it needs to be the one who is most likely to be influenced by the parents. Keep this in mind when dealing with schoolwide situations too.

If we contact all five students' parents and it does not have the desired effect of changing the students' behaviors, potentially we have bonded the five students against us, which we do not want to happen. Now, if it does have the hoped-for impact, then that is great. However, carefully think through your students. Is there a chance these five could be bonded against you? If so, proceed with great caution.

One suggestion might be to call just one parent. Keep in mind our goal is to go from five to four. Making sure you always have a strategy is essential in improving student behavior when utilizing parent contact.

The Peak of Ready

One other reminder that applies to administrators just as it does to our teachers is that we may be tempted to wait and build up our courage to call or contact a parent. We can hope it goes away on its own. However, many times when we do this, we worry and fret. Then sometimes we wait long enough and the student has arrived at home or called or texted their parent and then the angry parent contacts us. Now, what do we do?!

What has happened is by stalling, we are letting parents contact us when they are at their highest point of anger. They are the most prepared to be upset and let off steam. They are at what I like to call, the "peak of ready." They are at the point of being most upset and confident when they contact you. Even if earlier in the day, you were not positive what you were going to say to them and you may not have been your best, neither were they. Think about how you feel when you get caught off guard and how inadequately prepared you feel to deal with the situation. This same advantage can be yours when *you* initiate the contact before the parent is dug in and fired up. Though by initiating contact, you are not 100 percent at your "peak of ready," you pretty much guarantee that they will not be either. And if you call these volatile or challenging parents at work or at some other location when they may not feel as comfortable being verbose or disrespectful on the phone to you, it may further enable you to have a healthier and more productive conversation with them.

By being the initiator, you can make contact when you are ready, not when they are ready. Again, if you email bad news the parent now is able to fire back a response when they are at their prime "peak of ready" moment!

As school leaders, we must continually model for and teach appropriate interactions to our staff. Rather than just doing these things privately, it can be very beneficial for you to share with the faculty how you make decisions involving parent contact and the rationale behind it. Many teachers may not have discovered the idea of contacting one parent rather than all five, or initiating contact before the student arrives home or texts/calls the parent themselves. By using these approaches and then sharing them with others, the building leader can defuse many potential situations at the most appropriate point.

Chapter 4 Recap

- ♦ Communicate with parents more effectively by focusing on what you do know, rather than harping on situations where you both weren't present.

- ♦ Help teachers learn *which* parents to call when the class is out of control.

- ♦ Show teachers how to take advantage of the "peak of ready" strategy.

5

Dealing from the Role of the Leader

In Chapter 14 of *Dealing with Difficult Parents*, we looked at some strategies that will help teachers handle challenging parents. For example, we discussed how helping parents feel that we are on their side and that we are "giving them a good deal" can often help us forge a relationship with them or at least calm them down. These strategies can be utilized even more by a school leader.

As a principal, I used this approach successfully when dealing with challenging parents. I remember once that I had a new assistant principal, and a parent came into the office complaining very loudly that his child had been treated unfairly. This parent was offensive, rude, and overbearing—quite a pleasant trifecta. Anyhow, I went out in the main office area and asked the parent if I could help him. The parent went on to complain that his child had been suspended by the assistant principal, Mr. Johnson, for three days, and that it was not fair. I invited this parent into my office, and he bellowed on about how unfair a three-day suspension was for his son.

I lowered my voice, talked in the slowest and quietest tone I could, and asked the parent to tell me what happened. He described what his son had been accused of doing and continually refocused on the fact that the punishment his son received (the three-day suspension) from the assistant principal was unfair. Finally, again in the calmest voice I could muster, I said to the parent, "I had not heard about this situation until just now, but it does sound unfair." The parent relaxed and started to get a smug look on his face. I then continued.

"I'll have to look into this, but it sounds to me like Mr. Johnson did not handle this correctly." The parent continued to get a very satisfied expression. I then added very nicely, but firmly, "No, this doesn't sound fair. It sounds like your son should have been suspended for five days. As a matter of fact, I can make sure, because you seemed so unhappy with him, that Mr. Johnson doesn't deal with your son in the future." Then, before the parent could interrupt, I continued with, "If you would like, I will look into this tomorrow, and I will not allow Mr. Johnson to be involved. It sounds like he was really trying to work with you and your son by only giving him a three-day out. However, as I said, if you would like me to, I'll visit with the people involved tomorrow and I'll call you with the results. Since your son is already going to be home, I can just call you and add on the additional days. If you would like, I'll check into it first thing and give you a call as soon as I find out anything."

The parent immediately jumped up and said, "Well, you know, now that I think about it, I think that Mr. Johnson was okay after all. My son said he thought that Mr. Johnson was trying to be helpful, so I won't take up any more of your time. I think that Mr. Johnson was just doing his job, and I am sorry that I bothered you. Thanks for your help, but just forget that I ever came in. Have a good day."

It was amazing—this very belligerent parent went from insisting that this assistant principal was horribly unfair to thanking me and saying that he thought Mr. Johnson was bending over backwards to help his son. I guess maybe he thought that he got a "good deal" after all. Interestingly, this parent, who had a terrible reputation, never came in to complain again.

Principals can use language like, "normally this would be a 10-day suspension, but because . . . " or "We have had students removed from the team for the entire season for things like this, but since you have been so supportive . . . "

Dealing to Support Teachers

This exact same technique can be tremendously beneficial when you support your teachers. If the parents are upset that their child was referred to the office, and they feel that the teacher is "picking on them," one way to take the pressure off the teacher is to combine the concept of sharing what you know and also adding that you would have done more than the teacher did.

For example, in the previous chapter, we described a situation where the principal shifted the conversation from the current referral to something the principal had actually witnessed in the past. Here is a part of that example:

> However, I want to share with you what I saw your son do in Mrs. Martin's class last Wednesday. I saw him out of his seat, disrupting other students, throwing his pencil at someone else, and poking at three students with scissors. And Mrs. Martin did not send him to the office that day. You need to know I thought his behavior was so inappropriate that she should have.

One way to increase your support of the teacher is instead of saying, "I thought she should have," say "I would have." Say, "When I was in Mrs. Martin's class last week, I saw the way your son was behaving. If I were the teacher, I would have sent him to the office. Mrs. Martin has bent over backwards to do everything she can to be there for your son." That way, the parent feels like the teacher gave their child a better deal than you would have yourself. This can take the pressure off of the faculty member. It helps put the teacher in a positive light and can move some of the pressure off of him or her onto you. And as a leader, that is one important way to support your staff.

The Permanent Record

Being able to take a building-wide perspective can increase your success as a school leader dealing with challenging parents. When parents are upset their child is being suspended, you as principal can say, "Because you are supportive of our school and because you will have consequences at home, we will not put this suspension in your son's permanent record!"

What does that even mean? What's a permanent record? Who knows for sure? But that is an example of the advantage that the car dealer has. Knowledge. Whether or not suspensions are even recorded in a "permanent record" doesn't matter; what matters is that it seems like a carrot that is being offered to the parent to help calm the waters.

Keep in mind that you do not place all of the cards on the table at once. With challenging people, you must remain calm and lay your cards down one at a time. When one works, then keep the remainder of them in your hand for future use. This is one of the reasons you have to have the ability to control your emotions and thinking process, even when others around are not—*especially* when others around you are not. Once you use all of the tools you have stored up, they can become less valuable in the future.

Revisiting "Never Lies"

In *Dealing with Difficult Parents*, we use the all-too-true example of the parents who say that their child "never lies to us." As a principal, you are even more likely to hear that than the teacher is. If the first time you hear it, you blurt something out, then you are in a much weaker position and the parent is stronger. Remember that we want to ignore any tactic the parent uses the first time or two, to see if it goes away. If we have determined that it is a deal breaker and the relationship and conversation cannot go forward without resolving it, then that is when we want to use the tool.

In response to "he never lies to us," a principal needs to be able to say this: "What a special relationship you two must have. It is one I hope to develop with my own children. It is a priceless gift. We have been talking about having a series of parenting workshops in our district. Would you mind if I passed along your name as a possible presenter? That would be so powerful to have all parents build the open and honest relationships with their children that you have with yours . . . "

This can work for the teacher but it is easy to see it can even be more powerful when utilized by the principal. Not only does it likely put a halt to that silliness when the parent interacts with you in the future, it likely causes them great pause before they try it with faculty and staff members throughout the school. The other reason principals should be better at these things is because they get many opportunities to practice. Keep in mind that we must always keep a professional and sincere tone in working with parents. Any hint of impatience or sarcasm will often have a tremendously negative impact on the conversation and the relationship.

Upping the Ante—Please Don't Talk to Me Like That

In *Dealing with Difficult Parents*, one tactic we shared for dealing with a volatile parent was to calmly and gently say, "Please don't talk to me like that. I will never talk to you like that and I will never talk to your son/daughter like that. So please don't talk to me like that." If this is handled correctly, it works in pretty much every situation. It does not stop the dialogue; it just defuses the tone. If, as principal, you eventually have such confidence in the professionalism of your faculty and staff, you can even add to it. As a principal with an incredibly dynamic staff, here is what you could say to calm a very, very upset parent who was being incredibly rude toward you:

> Mrs. Smith, please don't talk to me like that. I will *never* speak to you like that, and I will *never* speak to your son/daughter like that. And, no one in this school will ever speak to you like that, and no one in this school will ever speak to your son/daughter like that.

You can understand why you could only do this if you have a truly professional faculty. Because if even one person in the school would yell or speak in an unprofessional tone, then you have not kept your commitment, and then the parents really do have something to be upset about. But if you can reach that point of professionalism throughout your school, it is another tool that can benefit you in dealing with the most challenging of parents.

Chapter 5 Recap

◆ Help parents see that you are giving them "a good deal." Use the dealing method to support your teachers, too.

◆ Try the "permanent record" tactic to further show you are doing parents a favor.

◆ Learn what to say to parents who claim their children "never lie" to them.

◆ Learn to tell volatile parents not to talk to you like that.

6

The Principal Must Focus on the Future

A principal's role is often a challenging one. We have to make some unpopular decisions. This is true in multiple aspects of the job. In working with parents, especially with unhappy parents, there has to be a way to solve or resolve the current issue and still work to maintain a future relationship. Keep in mind that no matter what negative thing occurred this time, none of us wants it to happen again. This is important for a teacher but is essential for a principal.

One component of being an effective building leader is to help your teachers look forward. Amazingly, students seem to be able to put the past behind them and approach class and school with a new outlook much more quickly than adults do. The best teachers are good at putting the past behind them, too. When a student misbehaves in the classrooms of the best educators, they want prevention. They want the behavior to not occur again. Unfortunately, in many schools, there are at least a couple of educators who take a different approach. When a student behaves inappropriately in their classrooms, they want revenge. They are much more consequence-focused than they are prevention-centered.

This same thing applies directly to parents of our students. Some of them want the situation resolved and hope to move forward and have their child make a better choice the next time.

Others focus much more on the details of what happened, what consequences the other students faced, the role of everyone else in the scenario, and even what happened to an older sibling or themselves when they were a student many years before.

There is no way to resolve these points of view. Instead, what we must be able to do is move their vantage point from the past to what lies ahead. It is easier to prevent an accident looking out the windshield than it is the rearview mirror.

Bus Discipline

Just hearing the term "bus discipline" can make even the best school administrators cringe. Having to defend situations that you have almost no ability to visualize is a tremendous challenge. Yet it is an important role in school leadership.

A popular children's song has a verse that goes, "The driver on the bus said, 'Move on back, move on back, move on back.'" However, nowhere in the song does a student say, "Why don't you try and make me!'" Thus, we know the driver was not the driver of a school bus. As assistant principal, one of my responsibilities was to handle the bus reports that drivers sent forward for approximately 600 eighth-grade students who rode the bus each day. Well, as you can imagine, this was quite a challenge. In addition to the 30-plus drivers having potentially varying skills, seldom did any of them actually observe the entire sequence of events that occurred to result in the students receiving a disciplinary bus "ticket." If we think managing a classroom is a challenge, just imagine trying to manage two entire classrooms while driving! Anyhow, what often resulted were bus reports that were potentially debatable.

The policy of the school district was that the first bus ticket was a warning, the second bus ticket was five days off the bus, the next ticket was 10 days off the bus, the next ticket was 20 days off the bus, and so on. The same consequence was to occur whether the student threw a paper wad, was out of his/her seat, or used obscene language to the bus driver. Not exactly the best policy to attempt to enforce.

One of the things that I quickly realized about these situations was that even determining exactly what happened would be difficult at best. Additionally, many times multiple students were involved, but the driver only reported one or a few of the guilty parties. Sorting this all out was next to impossible. However, I did learn that focusing on the future was a critical part of attempting to resolve the challenge of getting parents to be supportive. Let's look at a specific situation.

When I received a bus ticket, it listed the student's name, the offense, and the bus number. Typically, the amount of detail on the offense would be something to the effect of one of these terms: cussing, out of seat, yelling, rowdy, disruptive, and the like. Usually these tickets would arrive two to three days after the incident occurred, and the driver's ability to recall details were shaky, to put it kindly.

I would call the student down to the office and share that I received a bus report, and ask him or her to tell me what occurred. Sometimes the student would admit to something, but many times, it was a different interpretation than the driver had presented in the two- or three-word report. All of us have the skills to work effectively with students to get them to at least admit *some* possible wrongdoing. However, the real challenge was in contacting the parents. Here is how the conversation allowed for a focusing on the future.

> Hi, Mrs. Johnson. This is Bill Smith, assistant principal at Eastside Junior High. I am sorry to bother you at work but I wanted you to know that I received a bus report on Matthew for being out of his seat yesterday on the school bus. This is Matthew's first bus report, which is a warning. However, if Matthew receives a bus report in the future then it will result in a five-day suspension from the school bus.

Realize that what I did was get away from the details of this situation (which I seldom knew much about anyhow) and shift to the future. We would then have the typical discussion asking if Matthew had shared this information with them, and I would let them know that he was sitting right here if they would like to visit with him. Then I would once again look to the future to conclude the conversation.

Mrs. Johnson I would appreciate you visiting with Matthew tonight regarding the importance of proper behavior on the school bus, because as we had mentioned, if he receives a bus report in the future it will result in a five-day bus suspension, and none of us want that to occur.

A couple of things happened with this approach. We moved on from something I didn't really know much about—his bus behavior—to something that we could all agree on: that we did not want it to happen again. Additionally, if you think back to the discussion examining the car salesperson, the two things the parents remember are that this ticket is a warning and that the next one is a five-day suspension. And when parents hear the two terms, they realize that the warning sounds like a pretty good deal after all. Additionally, if you do happen to get another call from them, the parents already know the consequence. In the future, if there is another bus report, here is how the conversation goes.

Hi, Mrs. Johnson. This is Bill Smith, assistant principal at Eastside Junior High. I am sorry to bother you at work, but I wanted you to know that I received a bus report on Matthew for throwing paper yesterday on the school bus.

It is amazing how many times at this point the parent would interrupt and say, "I know, I know, five days off the bus."

Regardless of the parent's response, though, I would at some point reconvene the dialogue with, "As you might be aware, this is Matthew's second bus report, and the second report is a five-day suspension from the bus. However, if Matthew receives a bus report in the future, then it will result in a 10-day suspension from the school bus."

Then at some point I would conclude the conversation with, "Mrs. Johnson, I would appreciate you visiting with Matthew tonight regarding the importance of proper behavior on the school bus. As I mentioned, if he receives a bus report in the future it will result in a 10-day bus suspension and none of us wants that to occur."

And none of us did want that occur. Additionally, getting a five-day suspension did not sound as bad as what would happen next. Also, it made the future call easier if one was going to have to be made.

This exact approach is just as applicable from the standpoint of the classroom teacher, and principals need to ensure teachers use these practices when appropriate. Whether we initiate a parent contact or we receive an unexpected one, being ready to shift to the future can be very beneficial. Being ready with language such as "What can we do so that this doesn't happen again?" or "How can we work so that we have a different outcome tomorrow?" can be of tremendous assistance as we look to move the conversation off of the current situation where there may be little common ground to one where we are in agreement that we would rather not repeat the unpleasantness.

Chapter 6 Recap

♦ When speaking with difficult parents, try shifting the conversation to the future.

♦ Show teachers how to do the same. For example, they can say to parents, "What can we do so that this doesn't happen again?" or "How can we work so that we have a different outcome tomorrow?"

7

Always Show Concern

It is human nature to get frustrated when we repeatedly deal with the same students who misbehave or with parents who never support the school, even when it should be obvious that their child is in the wrong. However, even during these difficult times, it is essential that we do not lose our professional and empathetic stance. There is no way of knowing what the students' and parents' lives are like away from school. Though we should not have to bear the brunt of their unhappiness, sometimes that just goes with the job. There are certain things we can do even in these most predefined circumstances that can assist in working with challenging parents.

Negotiating Zero Tolerance

One limiting situation that may seem common today is the use of "zero tolerance" policies in many schools. Some schools, districts, and states have moved away from this term, yet we still face many presubscribed consequences for certain misbehavior. This is a situation where there is a predetermined punishment required for a specific offense. Oftentimes it is most common when there are weapons or drugs involved.

Many times, this is very fair and appropriate. We may have a chronically misbehaving student who has literally reached the end of the option possibilities and their behavior is such that unfortunately, we do not have a way to serve them in our setting. It could also be students, who when in school, prevent learning for many others or lead numerous other students down a path they would not go without their presence. Many of the techniques we have described can still be applied. Keep in mind the importance of working to make parents feel that we are on their side. Let's see how this can apply to a zero tolerance situation.

If your school has a policy of a one-semester expulsion for drugs, then you can still work to get on the side of parents. How? You can do this by showing concern for the student's success, even in this challenging or seemingly hopeless situation. First off, you can always rely on using the technique of expressing your sorrow by sharing that, "I am so sorry this happened." Though you may not actually be sorry this student is being dismissed from the school, you are still sorry it happened, or else you could be putting your time and energy into something more pleasant and productive. Being able to empathize—and being viewed as empathetic—is very important.

Another point is to "focus on the future." This is described at length in the previous chapter, but the idea is to shift from what has already occurred to what it is we can do now. In other words, show genuine concern for the students continuing their education during the time they are out of your school. Suggest some other school settings that may accept them—either private or alternative public settings. Even if there is little chance that these schools will accept them (and of course, that moment may not be the best timing for you to share the unlikelihood of this), the parents and students might still appreciate your concern and ideas. There is no reason to leave anyone with a sour taste in their mouth. No one benefits from a revengeful tone. Though it might be a challenge, showing personal concern and interest can soften parents' ire.

It is just like being involved in interviewing prospective employees. Regardless of whether someone is your top choice, or is even someone you would consider hiring, you would want the candidate to walk away from the interview feeling good about himself or herself and feeling good about your school. Why would you ever *not* want this as an outcome?

Also, there is another selfish interest in this. If students are removed from your school but may eventually return, you want to do everything you can to keep them on track to move up grade levels. You may wonder why, but keep in mind that if you do not do this, then when they return, they will just be in your school that much longer. We always have to make sure whenever we communicate bad news that there is hope and a potential for better things in the future. Like the car salesperson, there is definitely some advantage in working to be on their side. This time, we might not close the deal, but we want to be set up to have a better chance in the future.

During times when it does seem like there is no hope to the parent and student, we probably need to have an even wider swath of tolerance toward accepting their frustration toward our school and us. We may think we may never see them again, thus we don't need to tolerate it. Since it really might be the last time we see them, it is okay for them to feel like they "won." Some fights are not worth winning and some fights are not even worth fighting. Plus, as we know, many difficult parents seem to always have more children that will likely be heading our way. You never know what the breakthrough conversation will be that leads to a better relationship, so you have to set a standard of consistently being professional. Difficult parents already know how to behave inappropriately, and sadly, their children—regardless of their ages—have had years to use this as a role model. If we do not provide an alternative and better example, there is almost no chance that their children can ever take a different approach themselves when they become parents. In many situations involving the most challenging parents, we have to remember that if we are not going to be the adult in the room, then who is?

The Last Word

Though we have said this many times in this book and in *Dealing with Difficult Parents*, remember to continually practice the apology and infuse it into your conversations. Whenever you feel attacked or feel there's nothing left to say, try saying, "I am sorry that happened," "I wish that hadn't happened," or "I am so sorry that happened." Doing so can often heal even the most challenging wound.

Keep in mind this is not an admission of guilt. It is also not a statement that says there would be a different decision or outcome if a similar event happened again with this student or with a younger brother or sister. But what it is saying is that you have an awareness that this may be a very difficult and/or troubling situation, and you really do have empathy toward the student and the student's family, even in this very challenging time and situation.

Practice the apology regularly, and it will become second nature during the most stressful times. It can also help you to develop your own mantras so you can practice gentleness in tone, body language, and mannerisms. This can help you adjust away from a defensive or aggressive posture that is seldom the best choice in volatile or emotionally charged settings.

Chapter 7 Recap

♦ Show concern for students' success even if your school has a zero tolerance policy.

♦ Practice the apology. It is not an admission of guilt but an expression of empathy.

8

The Fairness Doctrine

Principals have to make schoolwide decisions on discipline and other topics, and many people love to use the "F" word—fair—to challenge or complain about the outcome of those decisions. All of your responses should start with the same thing. Remember that when a parent says, "My child never lies to me," the best thing to do initially is to ignore it and see if it goes away. The same thing applies here. When a parent says, "This is not fair," do not pull the trigger on a defense mechanism and try to explain your rationale. Do not respond by asking why it is not fair. Those responses can just perpetuate the juvenile tone that was set by the parent and his or her comment. People who whine and complain often do so regardless of what the issue even is. That is their nature. It should not be yours. That is why you are the leader and they are not. Dealing with difficult people first requires that you have the ability to deal with yourself.

It Wouldn't Be Fair If

In *Dealing with Difficult Parents*, we describe several situations where a teacher is accused of being unfair. It could be as a result of a grade someone disagreed with, playing time on a sports team, or really almost any decision a classroom teacher makes. Usually, the first response should be to not respond. Then, rather than being defensive, take a more proactive approach. Try saying, "What wouldn't be fair is if I didn't do this." Or "I know you are concerned about being fair; that is why I chose this action." If the other person really cares about "fair," then using this term in your response should help quiet the storm. Unfortunately, we often discover the person was using "fair" as a weapon and it was not really something they cared about. They were not concerned at all about the world being treated fairly or equitably. Instead, as it turns out, they had no big-picture concern or understanding at all. The only person they were interested in is the one they see in the mirror. Knowing this may not calm them down, but it helps you get a sense of what their real issue is. And most likely that issue is that they do not want any kind of consequence or to be held accountable at all. And, as you know, not being consistent with them really *is* unfair. The problem is that only you know it.

As a principal, I would use this same approach. If a student was being suspended for a fight in the cafeteria, and the parents felt his punishment was unfair, I would apply the following dialogue.

> I appreciate your concern about being fair, because you and I have the same point of view that it is essential that all students, including your son, be treated fairly. It is essential that everyone in the school be treated fairly. And I know that you want your son to be treated the same as the other students in the school. So it is critical that he be treated the same as the 250 students in the cafeteria would be if they had been the ones involved in a fight. Since every student in the school has received the same punishment for fighting during the three years that I have been principal here, the only fair thing to do is to treat him exactly the same as every other student in the school. And, I would not want your son to be accused of not being treated fairly because of me not suspending him. And I sure would not want the other parents to think you weren't being treated fairly, or the other 250 students

who saw him fight ever accuse him of being favored or of not being treated in a fair manner. Thus, the only choice I have in order to be fair is to suspend your son. And I appreciate greatly your regard for every student in this school, including your son, being treated fairly.

You're Right, It isn't Fair; It Should Be a Five-Day Suspension

The example given earlier, of the parent accusing an assistant principal of not being fair when he suspended a student for three days, is a classic example of this approach. As principal, I was able to respond:

> That doesn't seem fair; it doesn't seem fair at all. Why don't you let me look into that? Typically, that is a five-day suspension. If what you are telling me is correct, it sounds like Mr. Johnson (the assistant principal) made a mistake. I'll tell you what; I won't let him deal with this situation. Instead, I'll deal with it. Go ahead and keep your son home for the three days and I'll call you tomorrow with the additional days after I look into it. It sure doesn't sound like Mr. Johnson was fair.

It is amazing that if you approach this correctly, the parents will think, with hindsight being 20–20, that Mr. Johnson was very fair. As a matter of fact, if they really thought about it, he may be the fairest person they have ever known! What this also does is show tremendous support for the assistant principal and allows him or her to be viewed in a much more positive light than they were previously.

Let Them See Your Support

As a principal, I would have liked it if no one were upset with me, but what I really needed is for as few people as possible to be upset with my employees. I would have always rather been seen as the bad guy myself than have the responsible and caring people in my school be seen that way. If a parent is upset, have it be on you rather than on someone else in your school. You are the leader and should be able to continue to function effectively under these circumstances. Part of your role is to protect those you work with. Also, do not be afraid to have your employees hear conversations like this. It increases loyalty significantly and makes them **feel** incredibly supported. That's what a great leader does.

If you are in a meeting with a teacher and parent, being supportive is incredibly important and essential. When a parent is critical of a teacher who does not deserve it, do not hesitate to jump to the teacher's defense. Say something like, "I have never heard a parent say anything like that about Mr. Johnson before." Or, "He is one of the best teachers we have in this school. I would love for my own children to be in his classroom." Those types of comments can do wonders to support and build a teacher's self-confidence as well as enhance the teacher's confidence in you.

When teachers are in these settings and hear you backing them up, they truly can **feel** your support. And as you know, rumors and stories get shared quite often in a school. In this case, the willingness of the principal to go to bat for the staff is a powerful way to build trust and interschool relationships.

Here is another strategy that is among the most powerful and one to save until it is really needed. It will work with our most challenging parents and will be especially effective in providing support for employees we want to protect.

If you have been a school administrator for any length of time, there is a slight chance that a parent has contacted the central office to complain about you or your school. Hopefully, this does not happen too frequently, but eventually (if not sooner rather than later!) it happens to the best of us. When this does occur, would you rather hear exactly what the central office said in the conversation with the parent, or would you rather know they supported you? Of course, the latter is what we all hope for. We want to **feel** supported. We want to know that the central office is on our side. Here is an approach that allows our teachers to feel supported by us just as we'd want to feel supported by the central office ourselves.

The Happen In

If a teacher comes to you and says, "Mrs. Frankenstein (a particularly intimidating parent) is coming in to meet with me after school," why do you think the teacher is sharing this with you? Well, it could be because he wants to inform you, since when Mrs. Frankenstein is in the building, who knows what will happen. Maybe he is just informing you. Maybe.

However, a much more likely reason the teacher is sharing this is because he is worried, intimidated by, or even afraid of Mrs. Frankenstein and how the meeting will go. So, how should you respond? If you have a reasonable level of trust with the teacher, you could say to him, "Forget Mrs. Frankenstein—she is so disrespectful and unreasonable. What do you want me to do?"

The first thing you've done is immediately shown the teacher that you are on his side. This instantly gives the teacher confidence. Many times this is all that the teacher needed, just like when a parent goes to the central office to complain, you just want some reassurance that the central office is on your side. You do not want, expect, or hope the central office is rude to the parent—how does that help anything?—you just want to know they are supportive of you over the parent.

Quite often, as a result of your unwavering and supportive comment, the teacher now feels capable of dealing with the challenging parent on his own. The teacher just wanted some reassurance from his building leader.

However, remember, this is Mrs. Frankenstein, so maybe in this circumstance the teacher needs a little more.

After you say, "What do you want me to do?" ask the teacher this, "Do you want me to be in there when she comes in? Do you want me to be sitting right next to you or do you want to keep your power?"

Most likely, the teacher will not understand what you are saying and will ask with a puzzled expression, "Keep my power? What do you mean?" So you explain it this way.

If I am sitting there when Mrs. Frankenstein walks in, it will look like we need both of us to deal with her. It may make you seem incapable of handling her yourself. It could come across as if it takes both mom and dad together to discipline our son. The challenge is it may make you seem weaker. However, she is a deal to work with so if that is what you would prefer I will do it. Another option might be for me to "happen in."

The teacher may not understand and ask what you mean by "happen in." Here is how you share a possible approach.

When Mrs. Frankenstein comes in to meet with you this afternoon, within the first two minutes I will "happen in" to the conference. I will pretend I am there to ask you about a field trip coming up next week. Now you and I both know there is no field trip next week, but Mrs. F doesn't. So I will ask you if it is Tuesday or Friday, and I want you to write down the answer. If you write Tuesday, that means that I do not need you to sit in on the conference. It is going better than I anticipated. Friday means please join us; I am about to vomit from nervousness.

I also assure the teacher that they do not need to memorize this. I then have them write them down in their plan book "Tuesday go, Friday stay," so that they don't panic and yell "Wednesday," leaving us both unsure of what to do.

When describing this possible approach, I also share with the teacher that if they say Friday, I will act like I am leaving, but I will turn around and ask if I can join the conference. Then I will go get a chair and pull it up (sidle) right next to the parent.

After I explain this, I give the teacher a choice. Would he rather me be there when the conference starts which may cause the appearance of them being weak and afraid, or would they rather me "happen in." Unanimously, it is the happen in.

Then when the meeting occurs after school, I still let the teacher lead the conference if at all possible. But my presence alone creates a different dynamic than what Mrs. Frankenstein was expecting. The teacher and I are always kind and professional, but we have shifted any discomfort from us to the parent.

One challenge to keep in mind is that we may not be able to do this with every teacher. Most of the time, we can with no problem, but we may have one or two that it does not work so well with. We will explain in the next chapter.

Chapter 8 Recap

♦ When parents use the phrase "that isn't fair" as a weapon, don't respond defensively. Try saying, "What wouldn't be fair is if I didn't do this." Or, "I know you are concerned about being fair; that is why I chose this action."

♦ When you're meeting with a teacher and a parent, express your support for that teacher in front of everyone so the teacher hears and feels your support.

♦ Try the "happen in" method to support a teacher when he or she is meeting with parents (rather than being involved in the conversation from the get-go, which can undermine the teacher's authority or confidence).

9

What If We Are Wrong?

Everyone makes mistakes, uses the wrong tone of voice, or is not completely aware of the facts before making a decision. These things happen. They are no fun but they do occur.

If the leader does these things, we can immediately repair the situation by saying, "I was wrong." By now, we are good at using language like "I am sorry that happened" and "I wish that hadn't happened." Saying we are wrong should not take too much effort.

The difference in the role of the principal and the teacher can be very dramatic in this circumstance. The principal may need to repair the situation *for* a staff member who was wrong. This can be easy if the staff member *wants* to repair the situation. However, it is much more challenging if the leader is trying to defend someone who consistently takes a wrong approach and then stubbornly resists fixing it. Are there any long-term solutions to this?

What If the Teacher Is Wrong?

One of the greatest difficulties administrators encounter is when a parent calls to complain about a teacher's alleged inappropriate behavior, and it turns out that the parent was right. These situations do not necessarily need to involve allegations of gross misconduct on the teacher's part. Instead, they can be simple situations like a miscalculated grade or a misplaced student assignment. The reason for the difficulty has little to do with the error that was made. It has a great deal to do however, with the challenge of supporting the teacher while acknowledging that the parent's complaint has merit.

This is still relatively simple to do with the majority of staff members. Effective people are quick to acknowledge their mistakes and then work to repair them. Some people feel so bad that they even ask if it is okay to make a casserole and take it to the family's house as a reconciliation gift. Just sharing the situation with these staff members is all it takes for them to restore a positive dynamic. It is also easy for a principal to continue to be supportive of the teacher because you are aware that the likelihood of it occurring again is minimal or almost nonexistent.

But the stress of a situation increases exponentially when we're dealing with a teacher who may not be as skilled, who may not have as much interest in repairing bad situations, and who may struggle with relationships on a daily basis. What do we do as a principal if we have to support someone who may not always deserve to be supported? What if it is a situation where there is not one parent, but many who are raising the same issue?

Our first thought would be to improve the staff member through conferencing, tough love, and the evaluation process. These are all legitimate options, of course, and are things to consider using. But what do we do about the short term? What do we do to handle the situation today when the parent is right and the teacher is wrong but does not seem to have any interest in making a change? Is there a possible solution? What do we do to keep the parent—who is not inherently difficult—from becoming difficult because of the situation or because of something a teacher is doing?

Complaints about a Grade

Most every principal has parents who watch over their child's grades like hawks. They examine every paper, rescore every test, and challenge each judgment decision their children's teacher uses in grading. Potentially the same parents have a hand—or two—in their child's science fair project, biology report, etc. We appreciate parents who are concerned about their child's progress, but we probably are also aware that some cross the line.

However, what if parents are regularly raising concerns about one particular teacher, and the parents are doing so in a reasonable and professional manner? What then? Let's look at a scenario and then you can think through how you could take a similar approach with whatever issues you might be facing with parents.

Mrs. Starr is the nicest and most responsible parent in your school. Her youngest of seven is in his final year in your school. She has never complained about any teacher or situation involving any of her seven children. All of them are responsible kids and excellent students. She has asked to meet with you and Mr. Morose, who is her son's science teacher. Mr. Morose has multiple parents, over many years who have had concerns about his attitude, teaching approaches, and grading practices. Their biggest concern usually involves the fact that they get no warning regarding their child's grade in the class. They, and the students, are often times quite surprised when report cards or progress reports come out. Few grades are taken, and they are inefficiently returned to the students. Obviously, this is a bigger issue that would take more than one parent conference to handle. But guess what? The conference is in 10 minutes.

You, Mrs. Starr, and Mr. Morose are meeting about her son's science grade. Mr. Morose just keeps talking percentages and saying that it is her son's responsibility to ask more questions if he doesn't understand and that he needs to try harder. Everything he shares involves something the student needs to do differently. Naturally, you want to take the teacher's side, because after all, your instinct is to defend your staff member. But suddenly you get déjà vu. Parent after parent raises the same concerns, and Mr. Morose never takes on any accountability or responsibility for his teaching or his students. This is a tremendous parent, a conscientious student, and a teacher who regularly avoids effort. How can this be dealt with? Try this.

Say to the parent, "Mrs. Starr, what if on Fridays, if your son's grade is below a B, Mr. Morose calls you on your cell phone at 3:30 to share how Kevin did this week. He might share that Kevin did not bring in a homework assignment, struggled on a quiz, or missed some class participation points. This way you can know what Kevin should be doing differently to be more successful in Mr. Morose's class the next week. That way anytime your son's grade is below a B, Mr. Morose will call you on your cell phone at 3:30. What would you think about that Mrs. Starr?"

Of course, she would love it and would appreciate being informed about Kevin's progress in class. She wants to hold her son accountable, so hearing specific knowledge about what he has done or not done would give her tremendous guidance.

What does Mr. Morose think? He works very hard at avoiding responsibility and accountability. He has no interest in ever contacting the parent. What is the end result? He makes sure that Kevin's grade is always above a B. Problem solved—at least the immediate and temporary one. What is ironic is that everyone is on the same page. Mr. Morose never wants to have to call the parent. Mrs. Starr never wants to have to talk to Mr. Morose again, and Kevin never wants his least favorite teacher talking to his mom again. Win-win-win. Additionally, Mr. Morose may potentially do some self-reflection on his grades, if not on his teaching practices, just to avoid being in this uncomfortable situation with a parent in the future.

Who Is Difficult?

Leaders have to be supportive of their teachers and staff. It is a must. But at the same time, they have to ensure that the teachers and staff are doing the right things for the students in their classrooms and in the school. Otherwise, parents who should not be considered difficult become so. This is not because they are naturally tough people; it is because we are not taking care of their most precious commodity, the child they entrusted to us, in the way we should.

The best principals have tremendous loyalty to their staff. They know teachers are the ones who make the most direct impact on students each day. But the best principals also have tremendous loyalty to their students. That's why we have schools.

Chapter 9 Recap

♦ If your teachers are in the wrong, don't just turn to long-term strategies for improving their behavior. Long-term strategies—such as conferencing with the teachers, applying tough love, or addressing it during teacher evaluations—are not enough.

♦ Instead, help teachers in the short-term, through the language you use during parent-teacher meetings or calls. Make the teachers feel supported but still change their behavior so the parents who are "right" get what they need, too.

10

Build Relationships Before You Need Relationships

In several recent surveys of educational leaders, the one area in which many of them indicated that they would have liked to receive more training is interpersonal communication. Whether we are talking to a group of school administrators or a group of teachers, everybody seems to be increasingly recognizing the power of positive communication. The challenge arises when the individual or group of individuals we are communicating with is a difficult one. As everybody can attest to, it is far easier to communicate with a positive person than it is to communicate with somebody who is difficult.

Part II in *Dealing with Difficult Parents* has many ideas and reminders of how teachers need to work to build relationships. Of course, this applies equally to building leaders. Effective communication, we should know, must occur in good times as well as in bad times. If, for example, a principal is known to communicate with parents only when there are problems, then there will be a negative impact felt on the overall culture of the school. The school, as we have too often seen, will become mired in a culture of negativity. The norm will fast become one in which people dread seeing the principal at all. This is due to the fact that the principal has earned the reputation of being the bearer of bad news. A parent, already harboring negative feelings about the school or a school-related situation, will instinctively enter into conversations with such a principal from a defensive or aggressive stance. Either way, the parent will not be open to hearing what the principal has to say if he or she already expects it to be negative. The same can be said of every single staff member in a school. If a principal does make positive phone calls, send positive postcards and letters, and use social media to establish and reinforce trust and relationship, we are then required to have a skill set to continually navigate only negative parent interactions. It is imperative that we take a proactive approach to building trust.

What Message Are We Sending?

Remember when you first became a principal. Imagine your office and the physical arrangement in the room. You might recall the desk chair that you were given shortly after assuming the position. Well, it might not have been new, but at least it was new to you. The chair may have been a very high, executive-looking one, and, though the office may even have been small, sitting in that chair behind your large desk may have made you look and feel more powerful and imposing than you had ever looked before. With this in mind, what do you suppose would have happened if you sat in that chair behind that desk for all the conferences and conversations that took place in your office? Would people have felt comfortable and at ease in speaking with you? Would you have been more likely to cultivate positive relationships with parents, or would you have further established a wall that separated you and your guests?

There were times when sitting in your big chair and looking imposing may have served a purpose. Appearing confident and self-assured when dealing with a difficult or irrational person may have seemed like a good idea. At the very least, it may have given you a temporary shot of confidence. This being said, though, 95-plus percent of the interactions you have in your office should have taken place with you sitting in a smaller chair next to, or at worse, facing an individual in the same size chair with no desk in between you. Creating an equal playing field is vitally important in creating the kind of relationship that you wish to foster.

As leaders, we must help teachers understand this same dynamic. Do they try to meet in groups of staff when working with an individual parent? How can this make the parent feel, especially if the parent is in the meeting reluctantly? Do teachers call parents and personally invite them to back-to-school nights and parent-teacher conferences? If this is something that would be beneficial, it is important that the leader work to build the skills and confidence of teachers by developing and sharing language that everyone can use so there is a level of professionalism and consistency when initiating these parent contacts.

We also need to keep in mind what signage we have on the door greeting parents and other visitors. Is it welcoming or threatening? Do we have a friendly font or are there lots of **BOLD** words, *underlined* demands, and multiple directives with plenty of !!!!!!!!! at the end of our statements? Is this the message you hope to convey as people approach your school? If not, is it essential that you as the leader find a comfortable ground between establishing safety guidelines for guests and not kicking them in the shin when they approach your school.

Size Does Matter

We need to recognize that several structural difficulties exist in some schools that pose additional challenges to keeping parents involved. One difficulty is the actual size of the school. Without question, parents of children who attend very large schools often feel more intimidated by the school than do parents of children in smaller schools. There is also a tendency in larger schools for parents to feel as if they get physically lost. While these issues are real, and do affect some of our parents, they are not reasons to give up and conclude that larger schools can't possibly have strong parent involvement. In fact, many of the previously described ideas are regularly implemented in rather large schools. However, it's important to understand that larger schools can seem intimidating to parents. Once you understand it and decide that it really matters to you, then look for ways to effectively "shrink" the school for many parents. Breaking it up into smaller units (e.g., having a parent association for each grade level) is one way that school leaders have overcome this structural difficulty. For example, even very large high schools often have powerful parent booster clubs that are focused more narrowly on certain extracurricular areas and do not try to be representative of the entire high school community.

Another way in which some schools have chosen to address this obstacle is by implementing a "school within a school" philosophy. Larger schools are broken down into smaller units along such lines as grade levels or subject areas. Each of these smaller units is considered in many ways to be a separate school. The concept is similar to one that has been employed by larger universities for years. In these institutions, academic units are broken down into colleges or schools. Again, what is required by educators is an understanding that size can be an important structural barrier that many parents find intimidating. And this is more essential in situations where we're dealing with the least enjoyable parents.

Past Experiences

We may be dreading interacting with a parent because our history with this person has not been the most pleasant. This is a quite natural and understandable reaction. However, we need to remember that relationships, feelings, and potential baggage can go both ways. Challenging parents often had very unpleasant experiences themselves while attending school. Additionally, they may have had previous negative contact with administrators or teachers when some of the older siblings went through school. We need to keep in mind that the reluctance we may feel can be reciprocated, and sometimes the difficulty a parent may feel is related to a previous experience that has nothing to do with us. Making sure we do not take it personally or make it personal can help us change the dynamic to a more positive and forward-looking one. We owe it to the parents and owe it to the students. A new chance may be the only possibility of having a productive outcome.

Chapter 10 Recap

♦ Consider what messages your office and your school environment are sending to parents.

♦ Reflect on whether your past history with certain parents is preventing you from interacting with them effectively today.

Parting Thoughts

This book is not meant to serve as a be-all, end-all resource. The book *Dealing with Difficult Parents, Second Edition* is designed for all educators to draw from. Leaders need to be familiar with it because it can directly help them with language and scenarios that affect them and hopefully also provide support for teachers in working with challenging people.

However, the purpose for developing this supplement is to help administrators understand how the role of a leader is different than the role of the staff members in a school. As leaders, we have to support the people in our schools. Often we have to do so using only indirect knowledge. Sometimes we have to do so even when the employee did not make the best decision or use the best judgment. But that is an important part of what the role of the leader is. It is not just about doing what is best for yourself; it is doing what is best for everyone involved.

We also must keep in mind that the vast majority of the parents in our school are tremendously hard working, caring and loving people. They may not all show it in the fashion we wish they would. There are times their behavior is not the best, but they do have their own child's best interest at heart. The challenge we face as leaders is balancing the interests of everyone connected with our school and making it work best for every student. That's why we choose to lead. We want to make a difference.

References

National Center for Educational Statistics, School Nutrition Association. (2013). Online source: http://nces.ed.gov/programs/digest/d12/tables/dt12_046.asp.

Whitaker, T. (2001). *Dealing with Difficult Parents* (1st Ed.). New York, NY: Routledge.

Whitaker, T. (2002). *Dealing with Difficult Parents* (2nd Ed.). New York, NY: Routledge.

Whitaker, T. (2014). *Dealing with Difficult Teachers* (3rd Ed.). New York, NY: Routledge.

Whitaker, T. (2011). *What Great Principals Do Differently*. New York, NY: Routledge.

Whitaker, T. (2011). *What Great Teachers Do Differently*. New York, NY: Routledge.